On Your Mark
Take a Giant Step

Cover: Kelly Verret
Silsbee, TX
UNICEF Collection

On Your Mark

SCOTT, FORESMAN AND COMPANY • GLENVIEW, ILLINOIS
Dallas, Tex. • Oakland, N.J. • Palo Alto, Cal. • Tucker, Ga. • Brighton, England

Authors

Acknowledgments

Ira E. Aaron

A. Sterl Artley

Kenneth S. Goodman

William A. Jenkins

John C. Manning

Marion Monroe

Wilma J. Pyle

Helen M. Robinson

Andrew Schiller

Mildred Beatty Smith

Lorraine M. Sullivan

Samuel Weintraub

Joseph M. Wepman

Reader Consultants

Sally Joseph

Sue Wong

Pat Hutchins—pages 6–17
Kinuko Craft—pages 18–25
R. Masheris—pages 26–27
Dick Fickle—pages 28–30
Don Bolognese—pages 32–62
Dan Siculan—pages 63–64
Mae Gerhard—pages 66–80
Thomas O'Sullivan—pages 82–98
Don Smetzer—page 99
Abbott & Hollis Studio—pages 100–106
Grant/Jacoby, Inc.—page 107
Abbott & Hollis Studio—page 108
Dezso Csanady—pages 110–124

ISBN 0-673-10635-7   ISBN 0-673-10696-9

Contents

Did You Know?

About an Owl
by Pat Hutchins

Owl tried to sleep.
The bees buzzed,
buzz buzz,
and Owl tried to sleep.

The squirrel cracked nuts,
crunch crunch,
The crows croaked,
caw caw,
And Owl tried to sleep.

The woodpecker pecked,
rat-a-tat! rat-a-tat!
The starlings chittered,
twit-twit, twit-twit,
The jays screamed,
ark ark,
and Owl tried to sleep.

12

The bees buzzed, buzz buzz.
The squirrel cracked nuts,
crunch crunch.
The crows croaked, caw caw.
The woodpecker pecked,
rat-a-tat! rat-a-tat!
The starlings chittered,
twit-twit, twit-twit.
The jays screamed, ark ark.
The cuckoo called,
cuckoo cuckoo.
The robin peeped, pip pip.
The sparrows chirped,
cheep cheep.
The doves cooed, croo croo,
and Owl couldn't sleep.

Then darkness fell
and the moon came up.
And there wasn't a sound.

Owl screeched,
screech screech,
and woke everyone up.

How the World Got Its Color

adapted by Marilyn Hirsh

There was a time when the world was half finished. There were no colors anywhere except for a set of paints which the gods had given to an artist.

The artist painted every day while his daughter Miki watched him. As he used more and more color, each painting became more beautiful than the one before.

Taken from *How the World Got Its Color* by Marilyn Hirsh. © 1972 by Marilyn Hirsh. Used by permission of Crown Publishers, Inc.

One day Miki's father went to offer his best painting to the gods. He left Miki at home with her grandmother.

Her grandmother fell asleep, and Miki went to the room where her father kept his paints.

The colors were more beautiful than
anything she had ever seen. She stared at
them for a long time. Then slowly she
carried the paints outside.

She took a brush and painted the poppies
red, the trees green. The rooster wanted his
head to be red, and Miki painted the rest.

21

When Miki's father came riding home, she
was too busy painting her dress to notice
him.

When he came near and saw what his
daughter had done, he roared with anger.
All the earth shook.

The gods in charge of making the world looked down when they heard the artist roar. Miki was afraid, but when she looked up, the gods were smiling.

And as they smiled, Miki could see colors appearing all around her. Soon the whole world was colored, and it has been that way ever since.

What Is Brown?

Brown is the color of a country road
Back of a turtle
Back of a toad.
Brown is cinnamon
And morning toast
And the good smell of
The Sunday roast.
Brown is the color of work
And the sound of a river,
Brown is bronze and a bow
And a quiver.
Brown is the house
On the edge of town
Where wind is tearing
The shingles down.
Brown is a freckle
Brown is a mole
Brown is the earth
When you dig a hole.

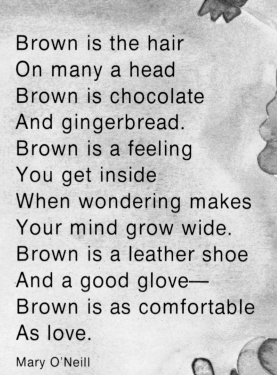

Brown is the hair
On many a head
Brown is chocolate
And gingerbread.
Brown is a feeling
You get inside
When wondering makes
Your mind grow wide.
Brown is a leather shoe
And a good glove—
Brown is as comfortable
As love.

Mary O'Neill

Brown is sad.
It makes me think of muddy shoes
Just waiting to be cleaned.

Robert Kerecz, age 8

How to Make a Palm Tree
by Patricia Palmer

You will need—
1 piece of brown
paper
2 large pieces of
green paper
a black crayon
glue
scissors

1. Use your crayon to draw
   the lines for bark on
   the brown paper.

2. Draw 16 leaves
   on the green
   paper.

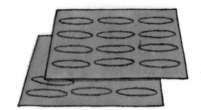

3. Cut out all the
   leaves.

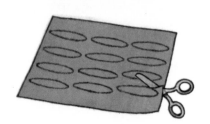

4. Put some glue along one long side of the brown paper.

5. Paste the long sides of the brown paper together to make a tube. This is the trunk of the tree.

6. Take 10 leaves. Make a fold in each one like the one in the picture. This will make a tab.

7. Put some glue on the inside of the tab of one leaf.

8. Paste the tab inside the top of the tree trunk.

9. Repeat steps 7 and 8 with the rest of the folded leaves around the tree trunk.

10. Draw a circle on the green paper. Make the circle smaller than the inside of the tree trunk.

11. Cut out the circle.

12. Paste the 6 other leaves around the edge of the circle.

13. Fold the leaves so that they point upwards.

14. Push the bottom of the circle of leaves into the top of the tree trunk.

That's Good, That's Bad

That's Good, That's Bad

by Joan M. Lexau

Bhai was just sitting on a rock in the jungle
when along came Tiger. "Run," said Tiger.
"And I will run after you.
And I will catch you.
And I will eat you. So run from me."

Bhai just sat there and looked at Tiger.
"Eat me then," said Bhai.
"I have no more run in me."

"Don't be silly," said Tiger.
"Why can't you run?
Tell me that, and then I will eat you."

"Well, it's like this," said Bhai.
"I was walking, just walking in the jungle
 when—bump!
I bumped into Rhino.

"Or Rhino bumped into me.
I was willing to forget it, but not Rhino.
He got mad, so I ran away from there fast."

"That's good," said Tiger.

"I ran and I ran and I ran and I ran,"
said Bhai.
"All the way, there was Rhino running after me.
He can't see very well, but
he can run fast."

"That's bad," said Tiger.

"So there we were, running along," said Bhai.
"Then I saw a low tree. I got up into it.
    Rhino was running so fast he went right by."

"That's good," said Tiger.

"Yes, but Rhino came back looking for me,"
said Bhai. "Oh! Was he mad!"

"That's bad," said Tiger.

"I got down and picked up a stone and threw it at Rhino," said Bhai.

"Good," said Tiger. "Good for you."

"It didn't hit him," said Bhai.

"That's bad," said Tiger.

"I ran again—not very fast. I was getting
tired, but so was Rhino," said Bhai.

"That's good," said Tiger.

"I ran and I ran and I ran,
with Rhino running right after me.
And then I fell," said Bhai.

"My, that *is* bad!" said Tiger.

"But Rhino was running so fast he went
right over me," said Bhai.

"That's good," said Tiger.

"As soon as I got up, there was Rhino back again," said Bhai.

"That's bad," said Tiger.

"I saw a vine on a tree, so I swung on it right over the river," said Bhai.

"That's good," said Tiger.

"And there on the other side of the river
was Crocodile," said Bhai.

"That's bad," said Tiger.

"So I swung back to the other side again,"
said Bhai. "I jumped off the vine."

"That's good," said Tiger.

"I didn't see Rhino—not right away,
that is," said Bhai.
"Then I saw that I was sitting on his back!"

"That's terrible!" said Tiger.

"So I jumped off and ran in back of a tree.
I picked up a stone and threw it as far
as I could," said Bhai.
"You know Rhino can't see very well.
But he heard the stone fall, and
he went running after it."

"That's good," said Tiger.
"Then you ran, and you got away from Rhino."

"Oh, no," said Bhai.
"I was too tired to go away.
 I just sat here."

"But—" said Tiger.

"And here comes Rhino now," said Bhai.

He got in back of the rock and said,
"Here I am, Rhino, over here."

"Help! This is bad!" said Tiger, as Rhino
went after him.

"Oh, no, it's good.
It's very, very good," said Bhai.

He wasn't tired any more, so he
ran along home as fast as he could run.

Does It Fit?

When you are reading, you may come to a word you don't know. When this happens, read the rest of the sentence. The other words may help you think of a word that fits in the sentence. Let's try it.

We brought ____ for our picnic lunch in the woods.

Do these words fit?
hot   chew   and   quickly   about
No, none of them fits. They make the sentence sound silly.

How about these words?

a sandwich   a banana   milk

That's right; they all fit!

Read each sentence and the three words
below each sentence. Then decide
which word fits best in each space.

Once upon a time, there
was a ____ sad knight.
the   very   run

He could not ____
his sword.
king   for   find

The very sad knight
needed his sword to
fight ____.
sad   down   dragons

He looked ____ for it.
everywhere   end   elephant

Then the very sad knight
____ that it was at the
blacksmith shop.
raindrop   remembered   run

The Man and the Donkey

The Man and the Donkey
an Aesop fable

One day a man said to his son, "I'm going
to sell the donkey.
Put this rope on him.
We'll lead the donkey to town."

The boy put the rope around
the donkey's neck.
Then the man and the boy and the donkey
started down the road to town.

They had not gone far when they met
a farmer.
The farmer said, "Why do you walk
when you have a donkey to ride?
One of you should ride the donkey."

The man said, "You're right!
One of us really should ride."

So the man told the boy to ride the donkey.
The boy got on the donkey.
And then they went down the road.

70

Soon they met three old men.
One of the old men said, "Why do
you walk and let the boy ride?
You should ride the donkey.
The boy should walk."

The man said, "You're right!
I really should ride and let the boy walk."

So the man told the boy to get off
the donkey.
The man got on the donkey.
And then they went down the road.

Soon they met two women.
One of the women said, "Why does
a big strong man like you ride and
make the boy walk?
The boy should ride the donkey."

The man said, "You're right!
The boy really should ride."

The poor man didn't know what to do.
He thought and thought.

At last he decided that both of them
should ride.
So the man told the boy to get
on the donkey with him.
The boy got on the donkey.
And then they went down the road.

Soon they met a family.
The mother said, "Why are you so mean?
That donkey isn't big enough to carry
a man and a boy."

The man said, "You're right!
The donkey isn't big enough to carry
both of us."

Once again the poor man didn't know
what to do.
He thought and thought.
At last he decided that he and the boy
should carry the donkey.

So the man and the boy got off the donkey.
The man cut a strong branch from a tree.
He tied the donkey's feet to the branch.

The man and the boy picked up the branch
and put it on their shoulders.

Then they went down the road, carrying
the donkey upside down.

Soon they got to town.
As they walked along the street,
everyone laughed at them.

The man and the boy came to a bridge and
started to walk across it.
In the middle of the bridge, the branch
fell off the boy's shoulder.

The donkey fell into the river with
a big splash.

And that was the end of the donkey.

Poor man! He had no donkey to sell.
He had tried to please everyone, but he
had pleased no one. Not even himself.

Talking It Over

1. How did the man try to please everyone?

2. Do you think the man learned a lesson?
   Why or why not?

The Big City

Grown-ups Are Funny
by Lilian Moore

"Grown-ups are funny," thought Ramon.
"It's so nice here, and they want to move
to an apartment house."

"Do not be sad, Ramon," said his mother.

"But I like it here in grandfather's house,"
said Ramon.

"You will like the apartment house too,"
said his father. "It is nice and big, and
there are many, many apartments."

"Then how will I find my apartment?"
thought Ramon.

"Many people live there," said his Aunt Rosa,
and she looked very happy.

"But what if they're all grown-ups?" thought
Ramon.

Soon they did move—Ramon and his father
and his mother and his Aunt Rosa.
It was a sad day for Ramon.
When he said good-by to grandfather's
cat, Big Pedro, he wanted to cry.
Ramon put his arms around the cat and said,
"Good-by, Big Pedro. I love you."

Big Pedro said, "Mew," and rubbed himself
against Ramon.

The day they moved was a day of
surprises too.

The apartment house had four floors.
Ramon's apartment was 2A.
"I can find that," thought Ramon. "All I do
is go to floor two and look for 2A."

The best surprise was the children—lots
and lots of children.
Soon Ramon got to know them.

Jimmy lived on the top floor in apartment 4B.
Leon lived in apartment 3B.
Johnny and his sister, Lola, lived right
next door to Ramon.
And the twins, Sara and Sammy, lived right
under Ramon in apartment 1A.

There was always someone to play with.

Every day Ramon ran up to the top floor
and called for Jimmy.

Then Jimmy and Ramon ran downstairs
to call for Leon.

Then Leon and Jimmy and Ramon ran
downstairs to call for Johnny and Lola.

They all went downstairs to call for
the twins. And then they ran out to play.

Mr. Carlos took care of the apartment house.
He lived on the first floor with a big gray
cat that he called Missy.

Some of the children were afraid of the big cat.
When Ramon saw her, he thought of Big Pedro
and put his arms around her.

The cat said, "Mew," and rubbed herself against Ramon.

After that Ramon and Missy and Mr. Carlos were friends. Sometimes Mr. Carlos let Ramon feed the cat. Ramon loved Missy.
"I wish you were my cat," he told her.

One morning Ramon's mother took him to the
store to get sneakers. Ramon wanted to play
in his new white sneakers right away.

As soon as they got home, he ran upstairs
and rang the bell of apartment 4B.

"Hello, Ramon," said Jimmy's mother.
"Jimmy went down to call for Leon."

Ramon ran downstairs and rang the bell
of apartment 3B.

"Hello, Ramon," said Leon's mother. "Leon
and Jimmy went to call for Johnny and Lola."

Johnny and Lola had called for the twins.
But the twins were not at home now.

Ramon ran outside. He walked around looking for his friends. No one was to be seen.
"That's funny," thought Ramon. "Where is everybody?"

He sat down on the steps of his house, and that was where Mr. Carlos found him.
"Hello," said Mr. Carlos. "What are you doing out *here*, Ramon?"

"I came out to find somebody to play with," said Ramon. "But I can't find anybody."

"They are all looking at something," said
Mr. Carlos. Ramon jumped up.

"Looking at what?" he cried.

"Come and see."

Mr. Carlos went upstairs with Ramon right
behind him. Then Ramon saw his friends.
And he saw what they were looking at.
Missy was lying in a box, and right beside
her were three tiny kittens.

"Look at the little white one," said Jimmy.
"That's the one I like best."

"I like the black one," said Leon.

"And you, Ramon?" asked Mr. Carlos.

Ramon looked at the little gray kitten and
thought of Big Pedro. "That one," he said.

"How little they are!" said Sara.

"They will grow fast," said Mr. Carlos.
"Soon they will be getting into everything.
 After that I have to give them away."

"Give them away!" cried the children.

"I can't keep four cats," said Mr. Carlos.
"The black one is for my friend down the
 street. The white one is for my sister."

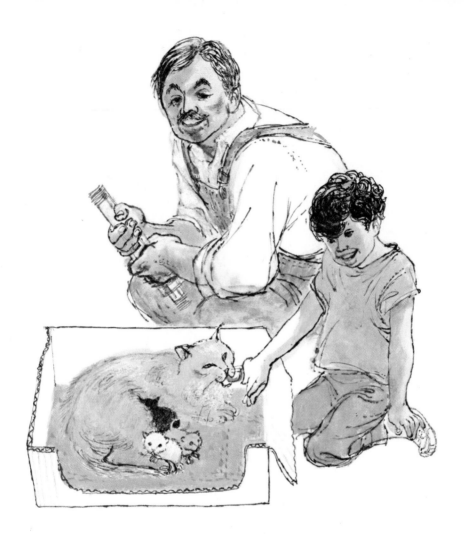

Ramon looked at the little gray kitten.
"And that one?" he asked.

Mr. Carlos laughed. "Missy says that kitten
is for Ramon."

That night Ramon told his mother and father
and Aunt Rosa all about the kitten.
"I'll call him Little Pedro," said Ramon.

"I will see Big Pedro soon," said Aunt Rosa.
"I am going back to grandfather's house
to live."

Ramon looked at Aunt Rosa in surprise.

"I do not like it here," said his aunt.
"An apartment house is too big.
Too many people!"

Ramon shook his head. "It's so nice here,"
he thought, "and Aunt Rosa is moving away.
Grown-ups are funny."

High Rise

Just think . . .

Your ceiling
may be somebody else's floor.

Your floor
may be somebody else's ceiling.

Their ceiling may be somebody else's floor.
Their floor may be somebody else's ceiling.

Et cetera.

Betty Miles and Joan Blos

Big-City Neighborhoods

Ramon's grandfather lived in one
neighborhood in a big city.

Ramon moved to another neighborhood
in the same city.

Grandfather's Home

A big city has many neighborhoods
in which people live and work.
There are buildings and streets and
people in every city neighborhood.
But the neighborhoods are not
all the same.

Ramon's New Home

This is one kind of city neighborhood.
Not many people live in it. But many
people come here every day.

There are big stores and places to eat.
There are many things to see.
And there are many places to work.

Many people work in this neighborhood too.
This is a neighborhood where lots of things
are made.
But most of the people who work here
live in other neighborhoods.

Some people live in neighborhoods
like this in a big city.
The houses were built a long time ago.
One family lived in each house then.
Now some of the old houses are made into
apartments where many people live.

Other people live in neighborhoods like this.

Many other people live in neighborhoods where there are high-rise apartments.

This is Ramon's neighborhood.

He lives in the middle of the block
on this street.

This is a map of Ramon's neighborhood.

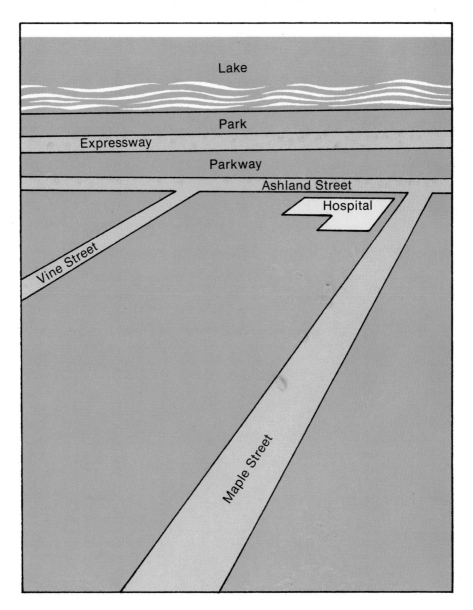

What is the name of the street that
Ramon lives on?

City Song

Many windows,
many floors,
many people,
many stores,
many streets
and many bangings,
many whistles,
many clangings,
many, many, many, many—
many of everything, many of any!

James Steel Smith

The House That Nobody Wanted

The House That Nobody Wanted
by Lilian Moore

There was once a little house that stood
on a hill. It was an old house—very old
and very gray. It had gray doors and gray
windows, gray walls, and a gray fence.

A little old man and a little old woman
lived in this house. And they had lived
there for a long time.

The little old man and the little old woman didn't go out much. But one fine day they made up their minds to visit their friends.

So they got into their little old car and rode away. They rode uphill and downhill and then uphill and downhill again.

And at last they saw the house of their
friends. It was a little red house with
white doors and windows, and all around it
flowers and green things were growing.

The little old man and the little old woman
had a good time with their friends.

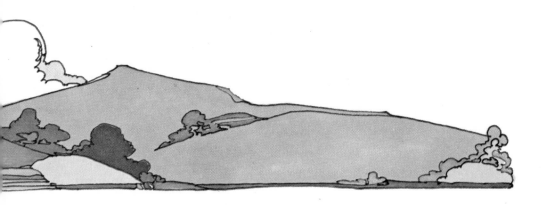

Then they got into their little old car
and went home. They rode uphill and
downhill, then uphill and downhill again.
And at last they came to their own house.

"My!" said the little old woman.
"Our house is *very* gray, isn't it?"

"And there's nothing green to see when we
 look out," said the little old man.

"Old man, let's sell this house!" said the little
 old woman. "Then we can buy a pretty house!"

"With grass and flowers growing around it!"
said the little old man.

So the little old man and the little old
woman tried to sell their house.

First, a man came to look. "No," he said.
"This house is too gray for me.
I like a red house."
And he went away.

"Oh, dear!" said the little old woman.

"Let's paint the house red," said the little old man. "Then maybe someone will buy it."

So the little old man and the little old woman painted the house red.

Soon after, a woman came to look. "I like
a house that has white windows and white
doors," she said. "I like a white fence
and a white gate too."
And she went away.

So the little old man and the little old
woman painted the windows white. Then
they painted the doors and the gate and
the fence white too.

Soon after that, a man and a woman came
to see the house. They liked the outside.
"But it's so gray inside," said the woman.
And they went away.

So this time the little old man and the little old woman painted the walls inside the house. They painted some walls yellow and some walls blue.

Soon another man came to see the house.
"This is a pretty house," he said. "But I'm
looking for a house with a garden."
And he, too, went away.

The little old man and the little old
woman began to work on a garden.
Soon green grass was growing.

Then one day there were flowers—red and
purple and yellow—growing all around
the house.

"Now someone will want to buy this house!"
said the little old woman. "Then at last
we can buy the house *we* want."

The little old man looked around.
"Old woman," he said. "What kind of house
do we want?"

"Well," she said. "We want a pretty house."

"Painted inside and out?" he asked.

"Oh, yes!" said the little old woman.

"With grass and flowers growing around it?"
asked the little old man.

"Oh, yes!" said the little old woman.

The little old man laughed. "Look around,
old woman!" he told her.

So the little old woman looked around.
She saw a red house with white windows and
doors, a white fence, and a white gate too.
She saw grass and flowers growing.
Inside the house she saw bright yellow and
blue walls.

"Well!" she said, surprised. "This is
a pretty house, isn't it?"

"This is just the house we want!" said
the little old man.

So the little old man and the little old
woman went right on living in the little
old house on the hill. Only it wasn't
a little gray house any more.

Talking It Over

1. Why did the little old man and the little old woman decide to sell their house?

2. Why did the little old man and the little old woman fix the house up?

3. What did the little old man and the little old woman do to their house to try to sell it?

4. Why did they decide not to sell the house after all?

Books to Enjoy

Gladys Told Me to Meet Her Here
by Marjorie Weinman Sharmat
Where is Gladys? Irving is supposed to meet her at the zoo. He is worried when she doesn't come.

Reproduced with permission from Harper & Row Publishers.

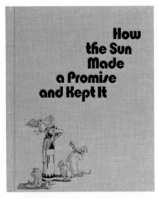

How the Sun Made a Promise and Kept It
by Margery Bernstein and Janet Kobrin
Do you know why the sun comes up every morning and goes down every evening? This old Indian story tells why.

Reproduced with permission from Charles Scribner's Sons.

The Lion and the Bird's Nest
by Eriko Kishida
Jojo was a lion who was growing old. He could not see very well. This story tells how Jojo and a little bird helped each other.

From *The Lion and the Bird's Nest* by Eriko Kishida, illustrated by Chiyoko Nakatani. Copyright © 1960, 1970 by Fukuinkan-Shoten, Translation copyright © 1972 by the Bodley Head, with permission of Thomas Y. Crowell Company, Inc., publisher.

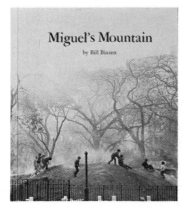

Miguel's Mountain
by Bill Binzen
Miguel lived in the city. One day some workmen left a big pile of dirt in a park. This story tells what Miguel and his friends did with the dirt pile.

Reproduced with permission from Coward, McCann & Geoghegan, Inc.

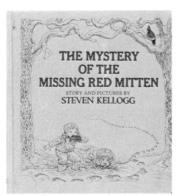

The Mystery of the Missing Red Mitten
by Steven Kellogg
Have you ever lost a mitten when you were playing in the snow? Annie did. Find out what Annie and her dog, Oscar, did when they learned that the mitten was gone.

Cover illustration of *The Mystery of the Missing Red Mitten* by Steven Kellogg, copyright © 1974, reprinted by arrangement with Dial Press.

Peggy's New Brother
by Eleanor Schick
Peggy had a new brother. But Peggy finds out that a new brother can mean lots of problems.

Reprinted with permission of Macmillan Publishing Co., Inc. from *Peggy's New Brother* by Eleanor Schick. Copyright © 1970 by Eleanor Schick.

Pet Show!

by Ezra Jack Keats

This colorful book tells about a pet show. Everyone but Archie had a pet for the show. Archie couldn't find his pet. What do you think he took to the pet show?

Willis

by James Marshall

Willis needed twenty-nine cents to buy a pair of sunglasses. His friends Snake, Bird, and Lobster wanted to help him. Guess how Willis got his sunglasses!

You Ought to See Herbert's House

by Doris Herold Lund

Herbert kept telling Roger about his wonderful house. Roger saw it, and so will you!

3 4 5 6 7 8 9 10 11 12 13 14 15 16 17 18 19 20 21 22 23 24 25 RRD 82 81 80 79 78 77

Take a Giant Step

SCOTT, FORESMAN AND COMPANY • GLENVIEW, ILLINOIS
Dallas, Tex. • Oakland, N.J. • Palo Alto, Cal. • Tucker, Ga. • Brighton, England

Authors

Acknowledgments

Ira E. Aaron

A. Sterl Artley

Kenneth S. Goodman

William A. Jenkins

John C. Manning

Marion Monroe

Wilma J. Pyle

Helen M. Robinson

Andrew Schiller

Mildred Beatty Smith

Lorraine M. Sullivan

Samuel Weintraub

Joseph M. Wepman

Reader Consultants

Sally Joseph

Sue Wong

"'Think of Tree.'" Text copyright © 1969 by Lilian Moore. From *I Thought I Heard the City*. Used by permission of Atheneum Publishers.

"American Indian Center." Photographs courtesy of The American Indian Center of Chicago, Illinois, and its Young People's Explorer Program.

"Turtle Rescue" adapted from "We Made a Home for Homeless Turtles" by Franklin Hoke. Originally presented in *Ranger Rick's Nature Magazine,* published by the National Wildlife Federation, 1412 16th Street, N.W., Washington, D.C. Reprinted by permission of the National Wildlife Federation and the author.

Photographs for "Turtle Rescue" courtesy of John Hoke.

Cover from *The Castle of a Thousand Cats,* text © 1972, by Harold Longman, illustrations © 1972, by Don Madden, an Addisonian Press Book, by permission of Addison-Wesley Publishing Co.

Cover from the book *Don't You Remember?* by Lucille Clifton. Illustrated by Evaline Ness. Illustration copyright 1973 by Evaline Ness. Reprinted by permission of the publishers, E. P. Dutton & Co., Inc.

Cover from *The Lazy Bear* copyright 1973 by Brian Wildsmith. First published by Oxford University Press, London, first American publication 1974 by Franklin Watts, Inc.

Robert Masheris—pages 6–17
Paul Hazelrigg—page 18
Nicole Hollander—pages 19–27
Brinton Turkle—pages 28–53
Ralph Creasman—page 54
Kinuko Craft—pages 58–80
Franz Altschuler—page 82
Arnold Zann—pages 84–98
Darrell Wiskur—pages 110–116
Sharon Elzaurdia—pages 118–130
Kawainui Kane—pages 132–151, 153–158

ISBN 0-673-10636-5

2

Contents

Times of Fun

All the Lassies
by Liesel Moak Skorpen

"I would like a dog," said Peggy.

"I know you would," her mother replied, "but we haven't room for a dog."

"Just a little dog," said Peggy.

"No," said her mother, "not even a little dog. How about a fish?"

Peggy named her fish Lassie.

She tried to teach it to come to her when she called. "Here, Lassie," she'd say. "Here, Lassie, old girl."

The fish swam round and round its bowl and didn't hear or didn't care to come.

"I would like a dog," Peggy said.

"I know you would," said her mother, "but we haven't room for a dog. If you'll stop pestering, I'll think about a turtle."

Peggy named her turtle Lassie.

She wanted it to wag its tail. "It's easy," she said.

But the turtle looked worried and drew its tail into its shell. The harder Peggy tried to explain, the more worried the turtle looked.

"I would like a dog," she said.

"Don't you like your turtle?" her mother asked.

"I like it very much," said Peggy, "but I'd rather have a dog."

"I'll speak to your father," her mother said. "Perhaps you could have a bird."

Peggy named her bird Lassie.

She wanted to teach her to bark. "Woof," she would say to her very clearly. "Woof, woof, woof." And the bird would chirp back at her with delight.

"No, Lassie," she'd say, shaking her head. "Not tweet, tweet. Woof, woof, woof!"

"I would like a dog," said Peggy.

"Oh, dear." Her mother sighed. She didn't say anything for a while. Then she said she knew about someone who had a kitten to give away.

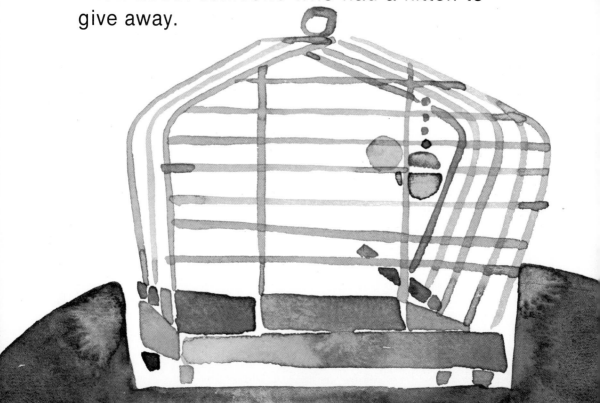

13

Peggy named her kitten Lassie.

"You must learn to chase a ball and bring it back to me," she explained.

The kitten loved to chase the ball, but she wouldn't bring it back. She batted it between her paws.

Peggy held her on her lap and stroked her head. "You're a very nice kitten," she said, "but you make a terrible dog."

Peggy's mother tucked her in. "I'd like a dog," she said.

Her mother sat on the edge of the bed and held her hand without saying anything. "Oh, well," she said finally, "perhaps a very small dog."

They came home with the largest, woolliest
dog in the shop.

The dog came when he was called, he
wagged his tail, he barked, and he brought
back balls.

Peggy named him Walter.

And he made very good friends with all
the Lassies.

Let's Play Ball!

Let's play ball! Let's play ball!   Come on

ev-ery-bod-y, one and all! Hur-ry to the park

where We'll play un – til it's dark there.

Come on ev – ery-bod- y, let's play ball!

18

Here's the ball! Here's the ball!
I will be the pitcher. It's my ball.
    First I'll try a fast pitch,
        And then I'll try a slow pitch.
Come on everybody, let's play ball!

Here's the bat! Here's the bat!
We will be the batters. It's our bat.

Can we hit a fast ball?
And can we hit a slow ball?
Come on everybody, don't miss that!

Here's first base. There's a mitt.
She can be the catcher. I can hit.
    She will be on my team,
    And I will be on her team.
We will make a great team. We won't split.

Let's take turns! Let's take turns!
Everyone can play then. Let's take turns.

Let's all play together.
We can have fun together.
Come on everybody, let's take turns.

"Batter up!" Hear that shout.
Will he get a home run. . .

or an out?

We'll all play together.
We'll all have fun together.
Come on everybody, come on out!
PLAY BALL !

The Boy Who Didn't Believe in Spring

by Lucille Clifton

Once upon a time there was a little boy
named King Shabazz who didn't believe
in Spring.

"No such thing!" he would whisper every
time the teacher talked about Spring
in school.

"Where is it at?" he would holler every time his Mama talked about Spring at home.

He used to sit with his friend Tony Polito on the bottom step when the days started getting longer and warmer and talk about it.

"Everybody talking about Spring!" he would say to Tony.

"Big deal," Tony would say back.

"No such thing!" he would say to Tony.

"Right!" Tony would say back.

One day after the teacher had been talking about birds that were blue and his Mama had started talking about crops coming up, King Shabazz decided he had just had enough. He put his jacket on and his shades and went by for Tony Polito.

"Look here, man," King said when they got out to the bottom step, "I'm going to get me some of this Spring."

"What you mean, man?" Tony asked him.

"Everybody talking about Spring coming, and Spring just around the corner. I'm going to go around there and see what do I see."

Tony Polito watched King Shabazz get up and push his shades up tight on his nose.

"You coming with me, man?" he said while he was pushing.

Tony Polito thought about it for a minute. Then he got up and turned his cap around backwards.

"Right!" Tony Polito said back.

King Shabazz and Tony Polito had been
around the corner before, but only as far as
the streetlight alone.

They passed the school and the playground.

"Aint no Spring in there," said King
Shabazz with a laugh. "Sure aint," agreed
Tony Polito.

They passed Weissman's. They stopped for
a minute by the side door at Weissman's
and smelled the buns.

"Sure do smell good," whispered Tony.

"But it aint Spring," King was quick to answer.

They passed the apartments and walked fast in case they met Junior Williams. He had said in school that he was going to beat them both up.

Then they were at the streetlight. Tony stopped and made believe his sneaker was untied to see what King was going to do. King stopped and blew on his shades to clean them and to see what Tony was going to do. They stood there for two light turns and then King Shabazz grinned at Tony Polito, and he grinned back, and the two boys ran across the street.

"Well, if we find it, it ought to be now," said King.

Tony didn't say anything. He just stood
looking around.

"Well, come on, man," King whispered, and
they started down the street.

They passed the Church of the Solid Rock
with high windows all decorated and pretty.

They passed a restaurant with little round tables near the window. They came to a take-out shop and stood by the door a minute to smell the bar-b-q.

"Sure would like to have some of that,"
whispered King.

"Me too," whispered Tony with his eyes
closed. They walked slower down the street.

Just after they passed some apartments
King Shabazz and Tony Polito came to a
vacant lot. It was small and had high
walls from apartments on three sides of it.
Three walls around it and right in the
middle—a car!

It was beautiful. The wheels were gone and
so were the doors, but it was dark red and
sitting high on a dirt mound in the middle
of the lot.

"Oh man, oh man," whispered King.

"Oh man," whispered Tony.

Then they heard the noise.

It was a little long sound, like smooth
things rubbing against rough, and it was
coming from the car. It happened again.
King looked at Tony and grabbed his hand.

"Let's see what it is, man," he whispered. He thought Tony would say no and let's go home. Tony looked at King and held his hand tightly.

"Right," he said very slowly.

The boys stood there a minute, then began tiptoeing over toward the car. They walked very slowly across the lot. When they were halfway to the car, Tony tripped and almost fell. He looked down and saw a patch of little yellow pointy flowers, growing in the middle of short spiky green leaves.

"Man, I think you tripped on these crops!" King laughed.

"They're coming up," Tony shouted. "Man, the crops are coming up!"

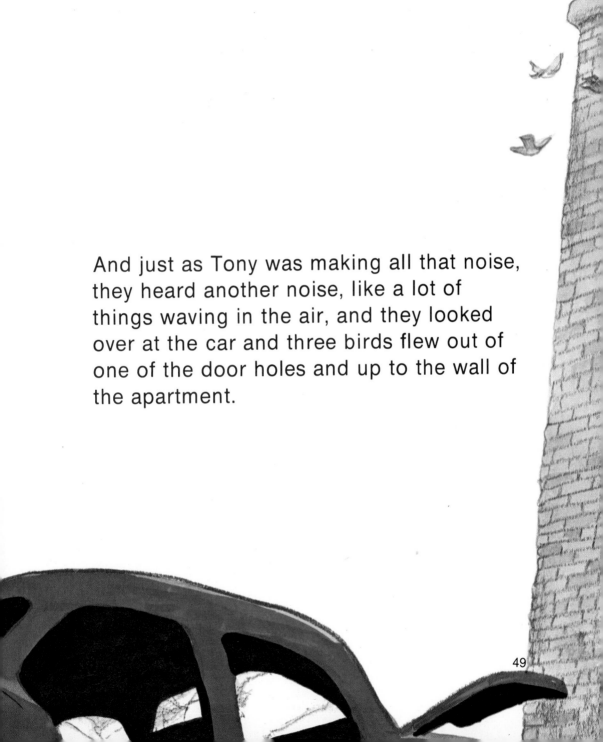

And just as Tony was making all that noise, they heard another noise, like a lot of things waving in the air, and they looked over at the car and three birds flew out of one of the door holes and up to the wall of the apartment.

49

King and Tony ran over to the car to see where the birds had been. They had to climb up a little to get to the door and look in.

They stood there looking a long time without saying anything. There on the front seat down in a whole lot of cottony stuff was a nest. There in the nest were four light blue eggs. Blue. King took off his shades.

"Man, it's Spring," he said almost to himself.

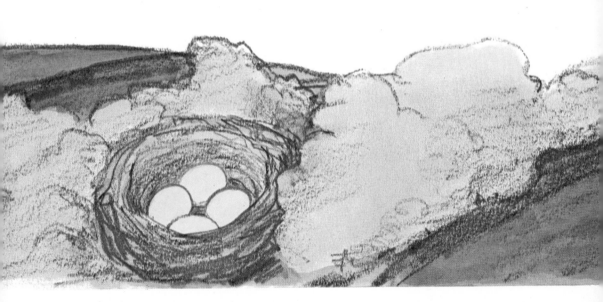

"Anthony Polito!"

King and Tony jumped down off the
mound. Somebody was shouting for Tony
as loud as he could.

"Anthony Polito!"

The boys turned and started walking out of
the vacant lot. Tony's brother Sam was
standing at the edge of the lot looking mad.

"Ma's gonna kill you, after I get finished,
you squirt!" he hollered.

King Shabazz looked at Tony Polito and
took his hand.

"Spring is here," he whispered to Tony.

"Right," whispered Tony Polito back.

"Think of Tree"

Under
the car smell

over
the tar smell

a sweet green and far smell
flows
down the street.

And it says
drifting by,
  "Think of tree.
  Think of sky.
  Think of ripe apples
  and hay, sun-dry."

Then you know—
not far away
they are cutting grass
in the park today.

by Lilian Moore

54

Does it make sense???

When you read, the words you know can help you figure out words you don't know.

Let's see how this works.

Read the sentences below and find the words that make sense in the blanks.

Amy's fluffy, little ＿＿＿ likes to purr. He purrs when ＿＿＿ pets him. He likes to sit on Amy's ＿＿＿.

Amy   kitten   lap   paws

Did you choose *kitten* for the first blank? Which words helped you know that *kitten* went in the first blank? Why does *Amy* make sense in the second blank? Why does *lap* make sense in the last blank?

After you read the sentences below, decide which words make sense in the blanks.

Ray liked to ride his new ____. He was mad when a tire went ____. He put ____ in the tire with a pump.

air   pump   flat   bike

How do you know *bike* makes sense in the first blank? Why does *flat* go in the second blank? How do you know that *air* goes in the last blank?

Read the sentences below. Decide which words go in the blanks and why.

Mary took her new tennis ____ to the park. She wanted to play a ____ of catch. She asked her best ____ to play with her.

game   rule   friend   ball

Then and Now

The Sunflower Garden
by Janice May Udry

Pipsa was an Algonkian Indian. She had five brothers. All the brothers except one were older than Pipsa. He was still a baby.

Pipsa's father was proud of how well her brothers could swim.

He didn't notice how well Pipsa took care of her baby brother.

Her father was proud of how well her brothers
caught fish.

He didn't notice how many berries
Pipsa picked.

Her father was proud of the way her brothers could trap rabbits and birds.

He didn't notice the baskets Pipsa had made.

Her father was proud of the first bows made by her brothers.

He didn't notice that Pipsa helped her mother make their clothes.

Pipsa's father taught his sons to do the things he could do. He often praised them. He never thought of praising a girl.

But Pipsa's mother was proud of her. Sometimes she said, "Well done, my little Pipsa!"

Every spring Pipsa helped her mother plant corn and beans and squash. How her brothers loved to eat! But they seldom helped with the planting.

This year, Pipsa was eager for planting time to come. All winter she had been saving sunflower seeds. At another village, Pipsa had seen the big sunflowers growing. She had tasted the delicious cakes that were made from the seeds. A girl in the village had helped Pipsa gather the seeds.

Now that spring was here, Pipsa planned to have a sunflower garden. No one in Pipsa's village had ever grown sunflowers. Pipsa would have to do all of the work herself. Her mother had all the work she could manage to do in the fields.

During the day Pipsa's brothers swam and fished and practiced with their bows and arrows. Pipsa and her mother planted and hoed. Gray Squirrel, the baby brother, toddled about close to his mother and sister.

The days grew warmer and longer. The only time Pipsa could work in her sunflower patch was after supper. She usually had to take Gray Squirrel with her and watch that he didn't wander away.

She looked down at the bare, flat ground where she had planted the sunflower seeds. She wondered if the seeds were really any good. Had she planted them right? Would they grow? Pipsa waited and watched.

Finally, after twelve days, the first tiny green shoot appeared. Soon the garden was full of little plants reaching for the sun.

It was a good summer for growing things. By July, the sunflower heads had many seeds. It would soon be time to pick the sunflowers and shake out the seeds for making cakes and oil. Pipsa had to watch Gray Squirrel because he wanted to play with the sunflower heads. He kept trying to pull them down.

As the seeds became ripe, Pipsa found that birds and mice began to eat them. So she spent as much time as she could guarding the sunflowers.

One evening Pipsa was chopping weeds away from the plants. Gray Squirrel was crawling around the big leaves. Suddenly Pipsa heard something. She stopped and looked quickly for her baby brother. Pipsa heard a rattlesnake!

She saw the coiled snake. It was the
biggest one she had ever seen! It was
lying in the grass. The baby didn't see the
snake or know what the sound meant. Pipsa
put her hand to her mouth. Then, picking
up the hoe, she crept toward the snake.
Pipsa knew she had to kill it before it bit
her brother. She had never been so afraid in
all of her life. What if she missed?

Pipsa hit the back of the snake's head as
hard as she could with the hoe. Without
stopping, she hit it again and again. Little
Gray Squirrel was very frightened.
He jumped to his feet.

"Run, little brother, run!" cried Pipsa.

Gray Squirrel ran crying to his mother.

Then Pipsa's mother and father and brothers
came running. Pipsa felt so weak that she
had to sit down. Beside her was the dead
snake. Everyone was surprised that Pipsa
had killed such a big snake. For the first
time she saw admiration in their eyes.
And for the first time Pipsa's father said,
"Well done, my little daughter. You are a
brave child."

Her father looked at the sunflower garden.
It was the first time he had been there.

"What are these?" he asked.

"Sunflowers," she told him.

"What are they for?"

Pipsa told her father that soon they would
have good little cakes from the seeds.

Pipsa's father asked her how soon they could have these things. He touched the big sunflower heads. He looked again at Pipsa with surprise.

He put his big hand on her head. "I am proud of you," he said.

The next day, her father told her brothers to take turns helping Pipsa guard the sunflowers.

Finally, Pipsa said that the seeds were ripe. Almost everyone came to watch her pick them.

Then they saw Pipsa pound the seeds into little cakes. She gave everyone a taste. They smiled and said how good the cakes were. Pipsa told them how to make oil from the seeds. She gave everyone some of the seeds. The next spring everyone in the village could grow sunflowers.

The whole village spoke proudly of Pipsa. She was the one who had brought a new plant and new ideas to her people. They called her the "Sunflower Girl."

As the years went by, the Indians in Pipsa's village grew more and more sunflowers. Pipsa had grown up and had a little girl of her own. The people often told Pipsa's little girl how her mother had grown the first sunflowers there. They told how she had given seeds to the rest of the village.

And Pipsa's brother, Gray Squirrel, never forgot that she had saved his life.

Talking It Over

1. Did the story "The Sunflower Garden" happen a long time ago? How do you know?

2. What were some of the things that Pipsa did to help her family? What were some of the things her brothers did to help their family? Why do you think Pipsa's father didn't notice many of the things she did?

3. What did Pipsa do that made her father finally notice her? What else had she done that made him proud? Why did Pipsa plant a sunflower garden?

4. Did the people of Pipsa's tribe think her sunflower garden was a good idea? How do you know?

Lullaby

Lullaby, little papoose,
Lullaby, little papoose.
Mother is near you,
Nothing can harm you.
Lullaby, little papoose,
Lullaby, little papoose.

a Sioux Indian song

"Lullaby" from *Music for Young Americans,* Book 3 by Berg, Hooley, Pace and Wolverton. Copyright © 1959 by American Book Company. Reprinted by permission.

Lull–a–by, lit–tle pa-poose,

Lull–a–by, lit–tle pa-poose.

Moth–er is near you,

Noth–ing can harm you.

Lull–a–by, lit–tle pa-poose.

Lull–a–by, lit–tle pa-poose.

American Indian Center

This is the American Indian Center in Chicago, Illinois.

Both children and grown-ups come here.

Some children live close
to the center. They can
walk there.

Others live far away, so
they come on a bus.

Here are some of the things that children
do at the center. They play games.
They paint pictures. They listen to stories.

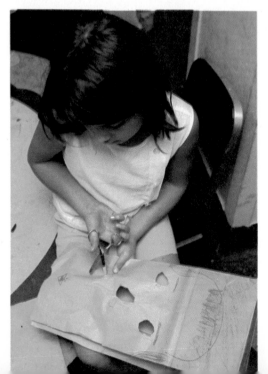

These children
are making
masks out of
paper bags.

One day these children took a bus trip
to the woods.

They saw many things along the way.

When they got to
the woods, they
ate lunch.

After lunch some
children went to
the lake.

Some children went for walks.

One boy climbed a tree. Another boy tried to catch a grasshopper.

Some children played games.

Then some children went over to the pump. They learned how to pump water.

The children found a good way to get a drink.

One girl found a good way to get cool.

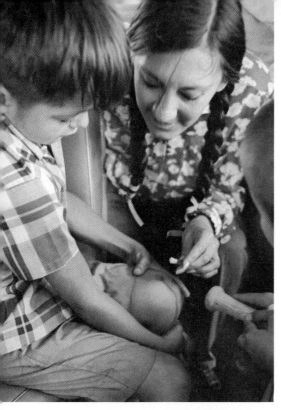

On the way back to the
center, a lady helped
a boy who hurt his knee.

Two boys went to sleep. Some children sang.
It had been a wonderful day.

Some nights grown-ups and children go
to a powwow. A powwow is a big meeting
where Indians get together to talk and
sing and dance.

At a powwow many Indians wear the clothes
that their tribes have always worn for
meetings like this.

The drummers make music.
Many of the people dance.

Everybody has a wonderful time at a powwow.

Turtles

"Turtle Rescue" was written by a boy named
Franklin Hoke. Franklin used the word I
in the article because he told about things
he did.

Turtle Rescue
by Franklin Hoke

I live near this canal. Men made the canal so that boats could take things from one town to another.

One summer men came to fix the canal. They let most of the water out. The canal was dry in some places. There were pools of water in other places.

Lots of turtles were left in and around
the canal. I knew that many of the turtles
would die before the canal was fixed.
So I decided to save as many as I could.
My brothers and sister helped me find the
turtles and take them home.

I made a home in a terrarium for some of the little turtles.

Other little turtles liked to swim, so I made a home for them in a plastic pan.

I kept some of the turtles in a plastic wading pool.

I put a log in the pool for the turtles to sit on.

I put a fence around part of the yard for the rest of the turtles. I dug a pond inside the fence. I put a log in the pond for the turtles to sit on.

Some of the turtles ate hamburger and different kinds of fruit.

Other turtles ate fish and different kinds of greens.

I kept the turtles until the canal was fixed.
Taking care of the turtles was a lot of work.
But it was fun too.

Talking It Over

1. Why did Franklin and his brothers and sister take the turtles from the canal?

2. What kinds of homes did they make for the turtles?

3. Why do you think they made different kinds of homes?

4. Why do you think they put the turtles back when the canal was fixed?

Kinds of Turtles

This kind of turtle snaps at moving
things. It's called a snapping turtle.

Snapping turtles live in ponds, lakes,
or streams. Their dark shells look
like rocks at the bottom of the water.

This kind of turtle has red and orange
marks on its shell. It's called a
painted turtle.

Painted turtles live close to water.
They like to swim. They like to sit
in the sun too.

This kind of turtle is called a box turtle.
It can close its shell.

Box turtles live on land. They live
in woods or meadows.

Talking It Over

1. Which of these is a painted turtle?
   a snapping turtle?   a box turtle?

2. How did you know?

You have read about some of the different places turtles can live. You also have learned what some turtles look like. The next story you will read is a Philippine folk tale about a turtle and a monkey.

The Turtle and the Monkey Share a Tree

edited by Harold Courlander

One day the turtle was sunning himself at the edge of the water. He saw something floating down river in his direction. When it came closer, the turtle saw that it was a banana tree.

From *Ride with the Sun: An Anthology of Folk Tales and Stories from the United Nations*. Edited by Harold Courlander. Copyright © 1955 by McGraw-Hill, Inc. Used with permission of McGraw-Hill Book Co.

He leaped into the water and swam out to the tree and pulled it to the shore. But he wasn't strong enough to carry it up onto the ground. So he went and found the monkey and brought him back to see the prize.

119

"Here is a banana tree I saved from the river," the turtle said. "Help me carry it to my farm, and I will plant it."

But the monkey was looking out for himself. He said, "If I do that, I deserve a share of the tree."

The turtle replied, "Help me, and I'll share with you."

So the monkey and the turtle together dragged the tree to the turtle's garden. The turtle said, "Now we will dig a hole to plant the tree."

But the monkey said, "Oh no, we said we would share."

"That's true," the turtle replied. "We'll plant the tree. When it gives bananas each of us will take half."

"Oh no, that's not the way to share," the monkey argued. "We'll divide now. You take half of the tree and I'll take half of the tree."

"It's a poor way to share a tree," the turtle replied.

"But, I want my share now," the monkey said. So the turtle cut the tree in half.

The monkey looked at the top half, with all the green leaves. It appeared to be the best part. He declared: "The top half is mine."

So he took the half of the tree with the green leaves away to his own garden and planted it.

The turtle planted his part of the tree and pressed the earth firmly all around it. The monkey's green half of the tree soon died. But the turtle's half, which had the roots, grew new leaves. In a matter of time there were bananas on it.

When the bananas were ripe the turtle wanted to pick them, but he couldn't climb. So again he brought the monkey and asked him to go up and throw the bananas down. He said, "For your help I will give you some of the bananas."

The monkey climbed. He sat in the top of the tree and tasted the bananas. The turtle stood waiting, but the monkey didn't throw the bananas down. He sat there eating them.

"Throw me some. I'll catch them," the turtle said.

"Never!" the monkey replied. "You cheated me before by giving me the bad part of the tree and now I am going to eat."

"Throw me a few," the turtle said.

"Here are the skins," the monkey said. He threw banana skins on the ground.

Now the turtle became angry. He went and gathered thorns from the bushes and scattered them around at the foot of the tree. Then he hid. When the monkey had eaten the last banana he jumped down and landed on the thorns. He danced around and shouted in pain. Wherever he stepped there were sharp points under his feet.

At last the turtle couldn't keep from laughing at the sight. When the monkey heard him, he ran forward and grabbed the turtle. He turned him over so that he lay on his back. The turtle was helpless.

The monkey then said, "Now you will be
punished for your crimes! Shall I beat
you with sticks? Or shall I throw you from
the top of a mountain?" And he made many
other suggestions of this kind.

The turtle said at last: "Yes, it would
be nice of you to do this. Throw me from
a mountain or beat me with sticks. Anything
will be satisfactory, as long as you don't
throw me into the water."

When the monkey heard this, he was delighted.

"Ah," he said, "the water! Why didn't I
think of it before? I'll finish you off in
the water!"

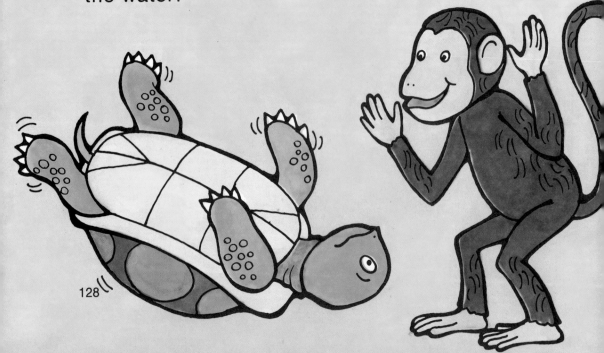

So he picked the turtle up, carried him to the river, and threw him where the water was deepest. There was a splash, and the turtle sank from sight.

The monkey was very pleased with himself.
But the turtle poked his head out of the water.

He said to the monkey, "Thank you, friend,
thank you! Didn't you know that the water is
my home?"

Hawaii, U.S.A.

Ah See and the Spooky House
by Vivian L. Thompson

It was a sunny day in Hawaii. Keoki ran
down the path from his house, past the
taro patch to Antone's house.

"Antone!" he cried. "You know the house
at the top of the pali trail?"

Antone rubbed his ear. "You mean the
empty one?" he asked.

"Yes, the empty one," said Keoki.
"There's somebody in it. Somebody who makes
   strange noises!"

Antone's eyes opened wide. "It might be
a giant!" he said. "Let's tell Saburo."

Across the river they ran to Saburo's house.

"Saburo!" Antone called. "You know that house at the top of the pali trail?"

Saburo rubbed his chin. "You mean the spooky one?" he asked.

"Yes, the spooky one," said Antone. "There's somebody in it. Somebody who makes strange noises! It might be a giant!"

Saburo's eyes opened wide. "It might be a ghost!" he said. "Let's tell Elmer."

Through the bamboo forest they ran to
Elmer's house.

"Elmer," Saburo whispered. "You know that
house on the top of the pali trail?"

Elmer rubbed his nose. "The one with the
high fence around it?" he asked.

"Yes, that one," said Saburo. "There's
somebody in it. Somebody who makes
strange noises! It might be a giant!
It might be a ghost!"

Elmer laughed. "Or just a family of mice,"
he said. "Little gray mice that scurry
and squeak."

"Let's go up and see," said Keoki.

Keoki led the way up the pali trail to the
house at the top.
It still looked empty.
It still looked spooky.
It still had a high fence around it, and the
gate was shut.

"I don't see anything," said Antone.

"I don't hear anything," said Saburo.

"But there could be something," said Keoki.

"There's a hole in the fence," said Elmer.
"Help me climb up, and I'll look."

Keoki stood under the hole in the fence.
Elmer climbed on top of him. He could just
see into the yard. There was something
there! It was looking right at him!

"What do you see?" called Saburo.

Elmer gave a yelp and jumped down.
"Two yellow eyes!" he cried.
"Big, wild eyes!"

"I don't believe it," said Saburo. "Let
me look."

Saburo climbed on top of Elmer.

"What do you see?" called Antone.

Saburo gave a yelp and jumped down.
"A long green head!" he cried.
"An ugly head!"

"I don't believe it," said Antone.
"Let me look."
He climbed on top of Saburo.

"What do you see?" called Keoki.

Antone gave a yelp and jumped down.
"A big, hungry mouth!" he cried. "With
sharp teeth and a forked tongue!"

"That's silly," said Keoki. "Let me look."
He climbed on top of Antone.

"Tell us what you see," called Elmer.

Keoki gave a yelp and jumped down.
"A dragon!" he cried.
"A big, wicked dragon! Run!"

Down the pali trail they went.
Through the bamboo forest—puff! puff!
Across the river—puff! puff!
Past the taro patch—puff! puff!
To Keoki's house—puff!

"It couldn't be a dragon," said Keoki.

"But it had big yellow eyes like a dragon," said Elmer.

"And a long green head," said Saburo.

"And a big hungry mouth with sharp teeth and a forked tongue," said Antone.

"Let's go back and look again," said Keoki.

Up the pali trail they went again, creeping softly this time, until they reached the house.

There it stood, empty and spooky. The gate in the fence was still shut.

Keoki whispered, "I'll look first this time."

Antone stood under the hole in the fence. Keoki climbed on top of him.

Just as Keoki looked through the hole, something went POP-POP! CRACK-CRACK-CRACK-CRACK! BANG!

Down came Keoki, rolling and tumbling.
Away went Elmer, Saburo, and Antone.

Someone called out behind them, "Come back!"

They were almost afraid to go back.
When they did, they saw that the gate in
the fence was open.

A boy stood there smiling at them.
He held a string of firecrackers.
"Don't run away," he said. "My name
is Ah See. I just moved into this house.
There was no one to play with, so I
lighted some of my firecrackers."

Keoki said, "Your firecrackers scared
us, Ah See. We thought you had a dragon
in your yard too!"

"I have," said Ah See. "Come into the yard."

Ah See led the way.
The boys followed—slowly.

Inside the gate they stopped.
There was a dragon!
He had a long green head, big yellow eyes,
a big hungry mouth with sharp teeth and
a forked tongue, and a long green body—
all made of boxes and cloth and paper
and paint.

The boys began to laugh.
"We thought he was real!" Saburo said.

"Where did you get him?" Elmer asked.

Ah See said, "My father and I made him for the Chinese New Year. We always had a dragon dance for the Chinese New Year in Honolulu, where we lived before.
Haven't you ever seen a dragon dance?"

"No," said Keoki. "Only a few Chinese people live on this island. We've never had a dragon dance here."

"Then we'll have one now!" said Ah See.
He closed the gate.

From inside came sounds of hurrying and laughing. Then everything grew quiet.

POP-POP! CRACK-CRACK-CRACK-CRACK!
BANG! went Ah See's firecrackers.

"Gung Ho Sun Nin!" he shouted.
"Happy New Year!"

Ah See opened the gate.
Out came the dragon, twisting and turning.
Down the pali trail he went, with Ah See
walking beside him.

There was no sign of the other boys. But
the dragon's first pair of legs looked like
Elmer's legs.
His second pair looked like Antone's.
His third pair looked like Saburo's, and
his last pair looked like Keoki's legs.

Gung Ho Sun Nin!

Talking It Over

1. Do you think the story title is a good
   one? Why or why not?

2. What did you like best about this story?
   Why?

*Ah See used to live in the city of Honolulu.
You will see photographs of Honolulu and
read about the city in this article.*

Honolulu

Most people who live in Hawaii live in the city of Honolulu. Honolulu has beautiful beaches. This beach is near the downtown section.

In downtown Honolulu there are many new buildings going up. On one of the buildings you can see the state flag of Hawaii flying under the flag of the United States.

Diamond Head Mountain can be seen from almost anywhere in Honolulu.

Banyan trees grow in the parks. Children like
to play on the trees.

Fish swim all year long in a pool in this shopping center.

Many years ago Hawaii was ruled by kings and queens. They lived in this palace in Honolulu.

Now Hawaii is a state of the United States. Honolulu is the capital of Hawaii. This new state capital building is across the street from the old palace in Honolulu.

Books to Enjoy

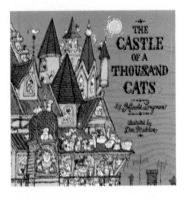

The Castle of a Thousand Cats
by Harold S. Longman
Miss Willoughby was rich and proud. She lived alone. She didn't know any of the poor people who lived near her. If it weren't for one small kitten, Miss Willoughby still might not know and like her neighbors.

Don't You Remember?
by Lucille Clifton
Tate was four years old, and she was stubborn. She knew what she wanted. She asked for it. But nobody ever seemed to do what she asked. Would anyone ever pay attention to Tate? Read and find out.

Dreams
by Ezra Jack Keats
When Roberto put the paper mouse on the window sill, he wondered what it could do. Later Roberto saw the mouse do something unusual. Did the mouse really do it or was it all a dream?

Reprinted with permission of Macmillan Publishing Co., Inc. from *Dreams* by Ezra Jack Keats. Copyright © 1974 by Ezra Jack Keats. British Commonwealth rights courtesy of Hamish Hamilton, Ltd.

The Lazy Bear
by Brian Wildsmith
The bear was good to his friends, and they all loved him. So the other animals wanted to please the bear. What do you think happened when the bear changed and wasn't nice anymore?

Lord Rex
by David McKee
Have you ever wanted something that belonged to someone else? Lord Rex the lion did. He even wanted to look like some other animals. Unusual things happened when Lord Rex started wishing for changes.

From *Lord Rex: The Lion Who Wished* by David McKee. Copyright 1973 by David McKee. Reprinted by permission from Abelard-Schumann Ltd.

The New Neighbor
by Florence Parry Heide and Sylvia W. Van Clief
The house next door to Eddie's had been empty for a long time. Then someone moved in. When Eddie saw the neighbor's wash on the line, he thought he knew what the neighbor would be like. Was he right?

Reproduced with permission from Follett Publishers.

3 4 5 6 7 8 9 10 11 12 13 14 15 16 17 18 19 20 21 22 23 24 25 RRD 82 81 80 79 78 77